THE
Dirty Beggar
LIVING IN MY HEAD

*One Guy's Musings
About Evil & Hell*

DON EVERTS

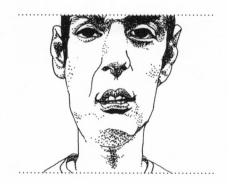

IVP Books

An imprint of InterVarsity Press
Downers Grove, Illinois

InterVarsity Press
P.O. Box 1400, Downers Grove, IL 60515-1426
World Wide Web: www.ivpress.com
E-mail: email@ivpress.com

InterVarsity Press® is the book-publishing division of InterVarsity Christian Fellowship/USA®, a student movement active on campus at hundreds of universities, colleges and schools of nursing in the United States of America, and a member movement of the International Fellowship of Evangelical Students. For information about local and regional activities, write Public Relations Dept., InterVarsity Christian Fellowship/USA, 6400 Schroeder Rd., P.O. Box 7895, Madison, WI 53707-7895, or visit the IVCF website at <www.intervarsity.org>.

Illustrations and design by Matt Smith

ISBN 978-0-8308-3613-0

Printed in the United States of America ∞

Library of Congress Cataloging-in-Publication Data

Everts, Don, 1971-
    The dirty beggar living in my head: one guy's musing about evil & hell / Don Everts.
        p. cm.—(One guy's head)
    Includes bibliographical references and index.
    ISBN-13: 978-0-8308-3613-0 (pbk.: alk paper)
    1. Devil—Christianity—Miscellanea.2. Good and evil—Miscellanea.
    3. Hell—Christianity—Miscellanea. I. Title.
    BT982.E942007
    230—dc22

                                                                    2007031457

| P | 15 | 14 | 13 | 12 | 11 | 10 | 9 | 8 | 7 | 6 | 5 | 4 | 3 | 2 | 1 |
| Y | 19 | 18 | 17 | 16 | 15 | 14 | 13 | 12 | 11 | 10 | 09 | 08 | 07 |

Contents

....

INTRODUCTION:
MY HEAD

....

Welcome to my head.

In the following pages I plan to introduce you to some of the various ideas that live up in my head. And you'll have the pleasure of meeting one odd idea up there in particular. That idea tends to behave kind of like a dirty beggar—hunched over all the time, eyes usually hidden away, looking down at the ground. This idea is wearing a dirty old robe and usually is sitting off by himself, his arms hugging his knees to himself, his eyes furtive. He's a shadowy kind of guy, dark and mysterious. THE DIRTY BEGGAR is what all the ideas up there call him.

But I'm getting ahead of myself. Before we meet this one strange idea, I think it's important to let you know why anyone should care about my head at all.

For the full answer, you'd really have to go on the full tour of my head.[1] But for now let me just say that my goal for trying to honestly describe what goes on up in my head (a potentially embarrassing endeavor) is not to provide some sort of intellectual peep show. It's really not. My first goal is to honestly describe what I believe about my own sinfulness and how that affects my views of evil in this world and the whole idea of hell. My second goal is to encourage more honest self-reflection and more relaxed conversations among people with heads full of different ideas. My hope is that my own honesty will help us all (myself included) practice the exquisite, everyday, joyful art of thinking more and more all the time.

That's why I'm letting you take a trip into my head to meet THE DIRTY BEGGAR. But before we get to the formal introductions, I should probably give you a peek into how things generally work up there in my head, so that this introduction of THE DIRTY BEGGAR makes at least a little sense to you.

Up in my head, ideas walk around like people.

Some folks say that ideas are inert propositional statements and that thinking is like doing science or math: you judge and weigh pieces of data until you find out what's consistent and true. Other folks say that ideas are more like snatches of visceral experience and that thinking is the act of honestly feeling these subjective experiences.

But when I am honest with myself, I have to admit that the ideas up in my head aren't quite so cold and datalike as some say, nor as subjective and experiential as others say. In my head, ideas tend to act more like people: they each have their own personality, their own style, their own way of getting along in my head. And each of them has a story to tell me.

For example, the dirty beggar that lives in my head is an idea with a story to tell about my culpability, or guilt, in this world and what that means about evil and hell. It's not like he's a dispassionate propositional statement about hell waiting to be examined or some existentially honest experience with evil waiting to be felt. It's like that idea is really up there. It has a personality and acts like . . . well, in this case, like a dirty beggar. A dirty beggar with a story to tell.

THE DIRTY BEGGAR isn't alone, of course. There are all kinds of ideas living up there, in this house of living ideas, and each one has its own story. Some have been up there since I was a kid (such as THE GOLD OF BOOKS, who tells a story about how great it is to be a reader); others are new ideas that walked into my head recently when I was reading a new book (for example, SHINY HAPPY GLOBALIZATION, who tells a story about the upside of our increasingly global economies and technologies).

That's what ideas are like up in my head. Thinking, then, is when I call a house meeting and all of the ideas (well, most of them) come to the living room in my head. The living room is where the ideas hang out together, tell their stories to each other, ask questions, argue, fight, agree and so on. Stuff you would do if you lived in a house with a bunch of other people and hung out together in the living room. When the ideas are interacting with each other in the living room—I'm thinking.

Sounds a bit chaotic, I guess. But if you've ever lived in a crowded house with a bunch of other people, you know very well that every house wants order. This order doesn't have to be explicit (*George is in charge!*), but it is definite (*George is a fifth-year senior?! I guess he gets the big bedroom, huh?*)

As in any real house, the house of living ideas in my head has social hierarchies (some ideas have been around longer and hold more sway), tensions (some new ideas that walk into my head aren't liked by anyone and are eventually kicked right out of my head) and complexities (not all the stories perfectly jibe, which means the ideas have some talking to do if they plan to live in the same head together). This is why getting the ideas to interact in the living room (thinking) is so crucial (and, usually, quite interesting).

Anyway, up in my head there is this one idea, called simply THE DIRTY BEGGAR. He lurks around, slouched over, and he has quite a story to tell in that haunting, hoarse voice of his. THE DIRTY BEGGAR's story is all about my own guilt and the spiritual realities of evil and hell.

But how did he get up there in the first place? And what, exactly, is his story? And what does he have to say for himself when other ideas start peppering him with questions? And, in the end, am I really going to let this dark idea stay living up there in my head?

Well, those questions are what this book is all about. Which means it's time to get on with the introductions. If you turn the page, you can enter my house of living ideas and meet this dark, profound idea for yourself.

Chapter 1

MEET THE
DIRTY BEGGAR

There is a dirty beggar living in my head.

And he's kneeling silently in a corner.

If you were looking around in my head, you'd recognize him if you saw him. *If* you saw him. He does keep to the dark corners of my mind. Doesn't interact with other ideas much.

His head is usually hunched over. His arms are often folded tight around himself, or sometimes I've seen him sitting on his hands and rocking back and forth. Come to mention it, I'm not sure I've really seen his hands more than once or twice. His fingers are quite thin, if I recall correctly.

He's dirty and he's dressed in a dark, baggy robe, like a depressed monk or something. Looks like he might have stolen several of those big hemp bags that coffee beans are sent to the local coffee store in. And made himself an ugly robe.

You won't see his eyes or face much either, but when you do, it'll send a shiver up your spine. Eyes

are wide and darting around the room, as if para-
noid. Bloodshot eyes too. Terrible to look at. His
face is all dirt like the bags he's wearing. All dirt
and maybe some ashes from a campfire some-
where.

And he rarely talks. A silent man. All bent over
and silent. Never looks you in the eye.

He will come into the living room of my head
and interact with other ideas from time to time. But
he is quiet usually. Sometimes during a meeting of
the ideas he may jump up in the midst of another
idea's story with his fists clenched and his eyes
wide. Then he looks around the living room at all
the ideas gathered there, and his face is serious and
even contorted. He stands there like he's got everything in the world to say. But his eyes usually drop
back to his own hands, to the ground in front of
him. And he sits back down again. Without ever
saying a word.

Other ideas in my head try to be polite, try to
cheer him up from time to time. "Hey, bud, why so
glum?" they'll say, patting him on the back as if trying to rouse him from a deep, disturbed sleep. But
he never wakes up from this shameful posture.

But sometimes (usually at night) I've heard him
whispering to another idea or two. He rarely offers
his story, seems a bit shy of other ideas. But at
times (usually when I am contemplating the darkness in this world) he can't seem to stand what

other ideas are saying and has an ugly outburst where he starts screaming and crying. Eventually he calms down and then has the gumption to tell his story.

His voice is hard to hear, though, and the two or three ideas sitting on the ground near him have to lean in to make out what he's saying. His voice is raspy and deep; it comes out hoarse, as if he's spent most of his life screaming or smoking. Or both.

And in the dark of night, in the silence of the darkness, he tells his story. Every idea has a story to tell. And this is how his story usually goes . . .

Chapter 2

THE DIRTY
BEGGAR'S STORY

If THE DIRTY BEGGAR living up in my head were a normal idea, you'd expect his story to come out nice and normal. But this dark idea isn't like most ideas. And so his story usually begins with screaming. Screaming followed by an awkward silence. And it's into that thick, awkward silence that he will tell his story. Whisper it, really. Whisper it in that strained, harsh voice of his.

This tends to happen on days when I am contemplating darkness. You know the days I'm talking about: the kind of days when something happens to make a person sit and think of this world. And think of the darkness and pain in the world. You know, something happens like traffic is backed up and I am late already, or the shocking acid of sickness or tragedy laps up against the safe shores of my life. And I start getting thoughtful about this world. And the darkness that is in it.

Darkness, evil, pain, brokenness—you can choose

your own word, but I think you know what I mean. THE DIRTY BEGGAR only seems brave enough to tell his story when I am thinking about this. THE DIRTY BEGGAR tends to tell his story on those days when I am listening to the news and the relentless headlines of horror finally push me over the edge and I find myself tired of the brokenness, tired of the destruction being worked on this beautiful, innocent planet. Tired of the wars and divisions and senseless violence that seem to be growing like a weed, a dirty weed that is taking over more and more human landscape all the time.

And in that fatigue I get thoughtful. I contemplate this darkness, this evil around me, and wonder what it is and why it is. And since thinking, up in my head, involves the interaction of lots of ideas, I call a house meeting and all the ideas up in my head start telling me what they think about darkness and evil. (Then I wait, bracing myself for the scream I know is going to come.)

At first some of the ideas in my head protest. WHAT A WONDERFUL WORLD, an optimistic and perpetually reminiscent idea, begins humming his tune about this great big, beautiful world we live in. He hums of beauty and loving interactions and sunsets that close calm days in beauty. "This isn't really a dark world," he assures the other ideas in the living room up in my head. "Babies are born and children play and waterfalls flow exquisitely and wheat grows steadily and is swayed by gentle winds—"

"In your dreams!" A usually silent idea, TRAGEDY, interrupts WHAT A WONDERFUL WORLD without apology. TRAGEDY is tired and all covered in dirt and maybe even some dried blood. He stares down this optimistic idea until IT'S ALL OK comes to his rescue. IT'S ALL OK is another perpetually smiling idea, a pleasant idea that always tries to bring calm and ease to the living room up in my head. Her voice is soft and convincing. "Listen, guys. There's no need to fight about this and go interrupting each other. It's fine. This world is still going to go on turning and people will still—"

And then she gets interrupted too. Maybe it's WAR or FAMINE or one of the many other ideas that have come to live within my head over the years that tell me, convincingly, of the brokenness of this world. Eventually WHAT A WONDERFUL WORLD and IT'S ALL OK quiet down and there is a general agreement of sorts as most of the ideas up in my head tell a story about the reality of darkness and evil in this world. And I believe their story.

And so I get along to wondering about *why* this is. Why the world is so broken. (And I brace myself for the scream that I know is coming.)

Why is there evil in this world? Why are there war and famine and racism? Why do kids tend to choose one child and treat him shamefully? Why do rapists rape and child molesters touch kids with thick, hungry fingers? Why do fathers yell at their children and kings ignore the needs of their people? Why do men pay to sleep with little girls and why does our government fail to prevent it? Why do we consume and consume regardless of what it does to the environment? Why do new regimes overthrow despots, only to become infected with power and harshness themselves? Why?! (I ask the questions and wait for the scream.)

Initially a robust dialogue ensues between PSY-CHOLOGICAL DETERMINISM and MY SUBURBAN BUBBLE.

PSYCHOLOGICAL DETERMINISM is a pretty sophisticated idea. He tells a story about how people are inexorably channeled toward each action they take. If people are mean-spirited toward their neighbors, this is because of their history: what they've been through has made them mean-spirited. "Why did that king become so callous toward the needs of his people?" he asks in his British accent. "Because he had no choice, because his life up to that point had formed him in such a way that this callousness, unfortunate though it may be, was inevitable."

MY SUBURBAN BUBBLE has a slightly different story. This calm idea speaks slowly, almost as if he's been drugged, about why there is darkness in the world. "Well, you see, there are mean people out there. Mean people who do mean things. This is why we are careful to lock our doors when we drive downtown. There are mean people out there."

His big eyes blink and the rest of the ideas in my head stare at MY SUBURBAN BUBBLE. He's got a bit of a gut and is dressed nicely. He smiles and continues, "This is why there is darkness in the world, because of the mean people out there. This is also why we should stay around good people, where there are nice lawns and smiling neighbors."

I tend to nod off when MY SUBURBAN BUBBLE speaks on in that slow, syrupy voice of his. But when I am contemplating darkness, he doesn't get to speak for long. Eventually he'll get interrupted by THERE IS A HIDDEN SPIRITUAL LANDSCAPE! This gal, wide-eyed and with hair that's messy, as if she's been holding her head in her hands, has her own story to tell. And she tells me that there is evil in this world because there are evil spiritual beings in this world. She rarely looks me in the eye, as she is continually, jerkily looking around her as if expecting to be attacked by a bird or something. "Listen!" Her voice is a fierce whisper, as if she is about to share the most important secret the world has ever heard. "There are spiritual beings all around us. And some of them are evil! Dark and evil and roaming around with ill intent, waiting to devour people."[1]

Her fierce whisper sounds important and I do

get roused from the slumber that MY SUBURBAN BUBBLE had lulled me into. And I like her story. Don't get me wrong—it is alarming. To think that spiritual powers that I can't see are affecting life? Creepy. And THERE IS A HIDDEN SPIRITUAL LAND-SCAPE! doesn't tell a story about cherublike devils up to mischief but about powers and beings that are much more subtle and sinister than that.[2]

After her story, I am alert and ready to listen to the different ideas up in my head and what they have to say about the presence of darkness and evil in this world I live in. THE SHODDY WATCHMAKER blames it all on God, and ORIGINAL SIN laments a disease endemic to all humans, and BLESSED CHAOS asks me why I would expect anything else, and WHAT HAPPENS ON OTHER CONTINENTS DOESN'T REALLY MATTER soothes me with words of calm . . . and then comes the scream.[3]

The scream. A shocking, desperate, ghoulish scream from an idea inside my head.

THE DIRTY BEGGAR has had enough. And despite his usual silence, despite his extreme shyness, he lets out a ragged roar that sends a chill down my spine. Even WHAT A WONDERFUL WORLD and IT'S ALL OK stop smiling. THE DIRTY BEGGAR screams again, though with less volume than the first time, and settles into a pained, twisted sort of crying. His dirty, robe-covered frame shakes as he cries. His face is entirely hidden in his arms.

THE DIRTY BEGGAR cries for quite some time. I wait patiently. I have the sense that this crying is the first part of his story. Every idea has a story to tell, and this, I feel, is an essential (if inarticulate) part of his story.

Eventually his crying and the shaking come to a stop.

And there is an awkward silence in my head then.

All eyes are upon THE DIRTY BEGGAR as he sits folded up and in pain in that ugly robe of his. And it is into this awkward silence that he finally musters the courage to continue his story. His eyes are still looking down, his face almost lost in shadow. But he begins to speak in a rough, exhausted voice. The ideas near him have to lean in to make out what he is saying.

"It was me." THE DIRTY BEGGAR's voice sounds harassed and exhausted. His head, still looking down, starts to nod slowly. "It was me."

IT'S ALL OK looks down at the pitiful idea before her, compassion and confusion in her eyes. She begins speaking in a soothing voice, "Listen, I'm sure that—"

"No!" THE DIRTY BEGGAR's voice rises high, his face still bent low. "No! It is not OK, do you understand?!" IT'S ALL OK looks confused and glances over at WHAT A WONDERFUL WORLD and then shrugs. THE DIRTY BEGGAR continues to nod slightly, his voice sounding tired. "It is most definitely not OK. There is darkness and evil. And it is because of me. I did it. I chose evil. I breathed the acid of evil. I breathed darkness into this world."

THE DIRTY BEGGAR goes into a coughing fit at this point, a rough smoker's cough, and the rest of the ideas living in my head are left either staring at this depressed idea or glancing at each other with confused looks.

PSYCHOLOGICAL DETERMINISM takes off his glasses and starts polishing them with his white shirt. "Young man, if you did indeed do some misdeed, I am sure that it was just because you were herded into such a decision. There's no sense in getting yourself all distraught over such an inevitable decision that—"

At this point THE DIRTY BEGGAR looks up (a rare occurrence), his face tortured, and stares at PSYCHOLOGICAL DETERMINISM. "I chose it. It was me." The words, short and sharp, come out like chops of a knife. PSYCHOLOGICAL DETERMINISM stares back, his glasses held still in his thin hands. "I chose it." THE DIRTY BEGGAR's stare only intensifies. "We choose what we do. In fact, I could choose to stand up, walk across this living room and punch your smug face."

PSYCHOLOGICAL DETERMINISM quickly puts his glasses on and backs up. "But . . . but you can't hit me; you're just an idea."

"An idea that's making a point."

EXISTENTIALISM stands, smiling, between the two ideas. He looks over toward THE DIRTY BEGGAR. "A point that is—?"

"That people choose. It's what makes them *them*. They could sit down or stand up. And some"—THE DIRTY BEGGAR looks back down at the ground, his voice seeming tired after so much talking—"some people choose evil. Subtle evil, big evil, funny evil. To have an affair, to rape a girl, to look with disdain at a neighbor, to claw at another person, another nation, this innocently spinning world. It's all darkness. It smells of vinegar and seeps around and grows and . . . and . . . "

THE DIRTY BEGGAR's head starts nodding slowly again as the ideas lean in to hear his raspy voice. "And it was me. I chose evil. And every choice has consequences . . . consequences . . . "

There's an awkward silence then. The ideas in my head aren't accustomed to such a dark idea. He just sits there rocking slightly, his arms holding his knees close to him, his face nearly buried in the folds of the robe. You can barely hear the words that come next. They are small words, but they hit the rest of the ideas in my head with the shock of icy water.

"And I deserve hell."

They are foreign-sounding words and make the rest of the ideas look shocked. A low murmur strikes up like a wildfire among the ideas in my head as they ask each other what he said and can barely believe what they are told. YOUTHFUL CYN-ICISM, a young, cocky idea who's not afraid to speak his mind, asks (louder than most), "What the hell is he talking about?!"

And THE DIRTY BEGGAR answers his question.

Chapter 3

THE FIST MUST FLY

THE DIRTY BEGGAR looks down at the floor in front of him as he continues with his story. Arms hugging his knees to him. He rocks slightly in his ugly brown robe as he talks, his voice low and deep, almost pained as it comes out . . .

"So I knew this guy once. Just a regular guy. Had a wife. And some kids. And a job. Just living right along.

"But he was one of these guys who looked forward to going home after work. Loved those kids and that wife. His favorite part of the day was walking in that door, letting his kids hear the door or hear his footsteps in the kitchen. Or just sense his presence. And they'd come running or they'd look up from their homework and give him those smiles. Favorite part of the day, it was.

"Some days, when work had been rough and his soul was all wrinkled up, he'd drive the long way home. So that his soul wouldn't be so wrinkled when he walked in. So he could take their smiles and breathe them in fully. He was a guy like that.

"He had this daughter, the youngest kid. She was his baby, I tell ya. A few years younger than the rest. And she was the last. The last baby. The last to learn how to walk. The last to fall down learning how to ride a bike. The last to thrill in her first day of school. And come home crying after a hard first day of school. And this guy I knew, he'd drink it all in. He just drank it all in—this little girl and her growing up.

"She'd sit on his lap as he read the paper at night in that rocker of his. And sometimes he'd stop reading an article about the wars in the world and the politicians' latest words and just feel her there on his lap. And look at that thin, long hair she had. And listen to her breathing. And he'd close his eyes then and feel the glory of her life, the beauty of her. He'd watch her thin fingers absently playing with the ripped fabric on the arm of the rocker. And when he went back to his reading, he'd read different, this guy I knew.

"So his kids grew up. And he kept working. And reading his papers at night.

"Even that youngest girl grew up. Her dreams and hopes grew up and she spoke of life in her own way and she went to high school and had friends and started wearing dresses that showed the shape God had given her and started going to movies on the weekends and wondering about college.

"One night, this guy I knew, he was sitting there in that tattered old rocker reading his paper. He was reading about the wars in the world and the politicians' latest promises when he heard his front door close, real quiet like. He hadn't even heard it open. So this guy I knew, he looked up above his paper at the door.

"His paper dropped from his fingers when he saw his youngest daughter standing there.

"He rushed over and scooped her thin body up and started yelling 'Mom!' louder and louder as he found his voice, and carrying his daughter, he walked quickly back to the bedroom where his wife was sitting, watching their small TV while folding some laundry.

"And this guy I knew, his hands were shaking as he felt the weight of his youngest daughter in his arms. His heart beat wildly when he looked into her dazed eyes. And his own eyes grew old when he saw the wrinkles in the yellow dress and the tear that had blood on it. And when she went into her mother's arms and began to slowly, deeply, quietly weep, he felt the glory of her and the beauty of her creation.

"He fell to his knees on their tan bedroom carpet, this guy I knew. And as he watched his wife holding his youngest daughter on their bed, the image he had seen when he looked up from his paper grew larger and each detail of it started etching itself, like a chisel into marble, into his memory. He saw her standing there. He saw the look in her eyes. He saw the way she held her hands. He saw the rip in her dress. And the fist in his stomach, that fist of the soul that we all have, clenched tightly and drew back as if to strike someone.

"He knelt there, father to a raped daughter.

"Father to a raped daughter. And his front teeth clenched together and his jaw drew tight. Each quiet, twisted sob that came out of his youngest daughter made the fist of his soul clench even tighter and pull back even further.

"And this guy I knew, he knew that the fist must fly. There was nothing mean or wrong or twisted in it. He felt the purity of the fist. His deep pain for the girl in her yellow dress, his compassion and love and the glory of her creation felt just as right and real and pure as that fist being pulled back in his stomach. And he knew the fist must fly. He knew the fist must fly. There was nothing twisted in that.

"This guy I knew didn't want revenge, didn't want to torture anyone. He had no energy for that. One blow was all it would take. And as he looked over at the glory of his daughter and her shaking, sobbing little body, he knew he must find the one who had done this to her.

"He knew it. And he was just a regular guy. I knew him.

At this point THE DIRTY BEGGAR living in my

head starts to speak more slowly, becomes even harder to hear . . .

"It's wrath. Wrath, you know. Pure and right.

"I have a sister, you see. Do you have a sister? Or a daughter?" His eyes look up sharply at the ideas around him, leaning in to hear him. He looks into their eyes—a rare, frightening occurrence—and holds their gaze. "If you have a sister, then you know it's pure. And right. This wrath. You know that the fist must fly. That choices have consequences.

"It's wired into the universe, into our skin. You see it in the glory of creation. I have a sister, you know. She has thin hands too, you see. And plays with the frayed edges of the arms of chairs too, you see. And if I just imagine . . . if I imagine the unthinkable . . . I . . . I feel the fist in my soul grip tight and pull back. It pulls back even to just imagine it.

"And God above. God above is . . . He is . . . " THE DIRTY BEGGAR's voice hesitates for a moment, and he seems to be collecting himself. "God above is Father to a raped daughter. And his fist must fly. It must fly because he watches each one grow up and feels each one on his lap and puts down his paper and just listens to their breathing and just breathes in the glory of each one. And his fist will fly. It will. It must. It is pure and righteous, this consequence, this fist. For he is a Father. A Father who loves, who sees, who is intimately connected and cares.

"Father to a raped daughter, he is." THE DIRTY BEGGAR looks back down at the floor in front of him. "And there is no place to hide."

THE DIRTY BEGGAR living in my head barely whispers at this point. The other ideas have to lean in to hear what he is speaking down to the floor.

"And I . . . and I . . . I did it. I have sinned."

His eyes are closed now. His arms are holding his knees close to his face, and he begins to rock and to speak with more and more force. It's almost as if he is going into a painful trance.

"And his righteous anger is a fist. The fist of eternity, the fist of a Father who has held his young daughter's raped body in his arms and carried her to the back bedroom of mourning and time and redemption. A Father who remembers. A Father who saw her come in and shut the door and hold her hands awkwardly and stare with that painfully twisted and glazed-over look in her eyes."

THE DIRTY BEGGAR holds his knees tightly to his chest and rocks back and forth and back again.

"A Father who hears each sob, who hears each sob . . . and even as one part of God holds and nurtures and weeps with a mother's arms and a mother's tears, another part of him kneels, collapses on the tan bedroom carpet and mourns and has a fist form within him. A right fist, a pure fist, a sure and strong and eternal fist.

"He knows, deep within, that his fist must fly. It

is a natural, pure consequence. He knows within that he must find the one who did this to his daughter. Every sin is a slashing, a clawing against one of his children. And he is touched intimately by it. He cares."

THE DIRTY BEGGAR's rocking back and forth starts to slow a bit. His eyes are still closed, his face still almost hidden as his voice fades.

"Hell is the fist of eternity. And it is due to me. I have no rebuttal, no defense. No need to argue. I did it. I have sinned. And this is my consequence."

RAPISTS
ONE AND ALL

After telling his story in the darker corners of my mind, THE DIRTY BEGGAR usually falls silent. He is completely bent over, his rough voice seemingly spent, his face hidden in the folds of his robe.

The other ideas living up in my head aren't sure whether they are supposed to ask him questions or not, his story being filled with so many odd elements, like that scream, and so much crying and lots of whispers. But the other ideas up in my head have their own stories, and many of these ideas (especially the newer ones in my head who haven't heard him tell his story before) don't like his story about the guilt and consequences of my actions at all.

And so, as ideas tend to do up in my head, they start interacting.

One idea up in my head acts as a watchdog of sorts, and he's suspicious of THE DIRTY BEGGAR's story. This idea, BEWARE OF HYPERBOLE AND EX-

AGGERATION FROM IDEOLOGUES, eyes him from where he sits. "Are you implying that the wrath of a human is the same as the wrath of God? That seems too simplistic for me. It can't be—"

"It's close enough." THE DIRTY BEGGAR doesn't even look up from where he's sitting. He seems fatigued from having spoken so much, being the center of attention in the living room up in my head.

A nearby idea, GOD IS LOVE, looks genuinely concerned for THE DIRTY BEGGAR. GOD IS LOVE is a strong idea (much stronger than GOD IS ALL CUDDLY AND AFFIRMING, a wispy, weak idea that rarely stays in my head for long). GOD IS LOVE looks over at THE DIRTY BEGGAR. "But why would God ever have a fist?" GOD IS LOVE is smiling. "His hands are busy serving and comforting, not hitting."

THE DIRTY BEGGAR doesn't bother looking up but does speak, his voice sounding fatigued from all the talking. "Where there is no love, there is no fist."

THE DIRTY BEGGAR breaks into another coughing fit and continues hoarsely. "You are right. God is not indifferent. He cares. He is a Father, after all. If he didn't care, then the darkness wouldn't affect him. But where there is deep love and deep hurt, there is a strong reaction. God cares when his children are hurt. Just like . . . a father."

GOD IS LOVE smiles a bit and nods at THE DIRTY BEGGAR. "Yes, I think you are on to something there about God caring and being compassionate—"

"Which means every sin, every dark claw that scrapes one of his children, means something to him." THE DIRTY BEGGAR is still bent over, his voice rough and fatigued. "He sees. He notices. And he cares. The fist in his stomach pulls back— because he has such love for his raped daughter."

Some of the ideas living up there (especially members of the Enlightenment Gang) try to cheer the beggar up. THE BEAUTY OF ACCEPTANCE puts a hand on his shoulder. "Listen, fellow. I'm sorry that you feel guilty about some stuff you've done, but it's not like *you've* raped anyone. Have you?"

THE DIRTY BEGGAR doesn't even look up, but he shakes his head and mumbles, barely audible. "No."

THE BEAUTY OF ACCEPTANCE leans in a bit more and talks in a sugary voice, almost as if speaking to a young child. "So, what's the problem? Listen, so maybe you've lied or cussed or hurt some people in your day. Nobody's perfect. We've all cheated on someone or been mean at times. But it's not like you're a rapist or a murderer. Don't worry, you'll get over it. You're fine."

At this point THE DIRTY BEGGAR looks up. His eyes are even more bloodshot than before and hard to look at for long. "Not a rapist?"

"Yeah. Nobody's perfect, but—"

"Not a rapist?!" THE DIRTY BEGGAR's eyes grow

even wider and his hoarse voice invades the hush in the dark room. "But we're all rapists!"

Many of the ideas in my head are not used to being called names by other ideas, especially not *rapists,* and the looks on their faces make it clear they are offended. The members of the Enlightenment Gang look especially wounded by his harsh words. THE BEAUTY OF ACCEPTANCE, ABOVE ALL NEVER JUDGE and POINTING IS RUDE actually get up at this point and walk away from the beggar living in my head. They shake their heads, clearly offended.

The ones who stay have their shocked looks met with another story told in the hoarse, pained voice of THE DIRTY BEGGAR. Many of the ideas sitting around him in the living room up in my head exchange worried looks as he continues in muttering, harsh whispers . . .

"Rape. Murder. Adultery. Lust. Deception. Selfishness. Indifference. What's the difference?! There is no difference. THE GRAND SPECTRUM OF SINS is an idea that has no place in this head—I had that fool kicked out years ago!"

The newest ideas living in my head are shocked at this. Some of them have never been in a head that didn't have THE GRAND SPECTRUM OF SINS living with them before. HUMANISM, the muscular idea who always wears a tight, one-piece outfit (something right from the set of the original *Star Trek*),[1] sees the nervousness in the living room and calls out from where he's sitting, "You can't mean that raping someone is no different from telling a lie."

THE DIRTY BEGGAR, sitting nearly hidden in his ugly robe, closes his eyes and his head drops. His tired, mournful voice rises after a few moments of silence . . .

"Listen, you can talk with THE OLD MAN CLUTCHING THE BIG BLACK BIBLE if you like."[2] There's a gasp of sorts at the mention of THE OLD MAN—who is never far away, since THE DIRTY BEGGAR doesn't like to stray far from him and his big black Bible.

THE OLD MAN is a Permanent Resident in my head. Though he looks stiff and outdated, he holds a lot of sway up in my head. He nods and gently touches the cover of his huge black Bible with his thin, vein-covered hands. He speaks in an ancient, somber, almost frail voice. "Jesus himself said that calling someone a name out of anger is the same as murdering him. He said that lusting after a woman is the same as committing adultery with her.[3] James wrote later on that if you sin against one part of the law—he was referring to favoritism toward rich people at the time—you have broken the entire law and are accountable for that."[4]

HUMANISM, TRUTH IS RELATIVE, POINTING IS RUDE and ABOVE ALL NEVER JUDGE stare at THE OLD MAN CLUTCHING THE BIG BLACK BIBLE as if he were crazy. THE OLD MAN takes the moment of silence as an opportunity to say more. He turns a few thin, fragile pages in his big black book and continues, "In speaking about sins, Jesus said that it was what comes out of a person that defiles him. For it is from within the human heart that evil intentions come: fornication, theft, murder, adultery, avarice, wickedness, deceit, licentiousness, envy, slander, pride, folly. All these evil things come from within, and they defile a person."[5]

At this point THE OLD MAN looks up from the black Bible. "Jesus spoke about sin as horrendous. For example, he said it's better to be drowned by having a huge millstone tied to your neck and being thrown into a deep sea than to cause someone else to sin.[6] Jesus spoke of the nearly unthinkable horrendousness of sin, but there's no indication of a spectrum of horrendousness at all."

YOUTHFUL CYNICISM rolls his eyes and looks back over to THE DIRTY BEGGAR living in my head. "You actually believe all this old Puritanical stuff? You've got to be kidding! Murder is obviously different from adultery. Which is obviously different from just 'lusting' after someone—as if that's even a bad thing at all!"

THE DIRTY BEGGAR nods his head slowly. "I do believe THE OLD MAN."

The beggar's simplistic admission causes lots of shaking of heads and rolling of eyes from many of the ideas living in my head. YOUTHFUL CYNI-

CISM's sarcastic voice can be heard all through my head cracking jokes about THE OLD MAN and his silly old book. But the mocking comments eventually die down as THE DIRTY BEGGAR's rarely heard voice begins to fill the living room with its deep, hoarse drone as he tells another story.

"I knew this gal once. She was a regular gal. Grew up regular.

"Like most little girls, she hunched over her diary in secret and wrote her deepest thoughts in it. She had a thin little key she'd lock it up with. She grew up with the normal dreams of a little girl. Dreaming of being a princess, of being treasured and protected and embraced as someone of beauty and glory.

"This gal I knew would always wonder—every time she met a new boy—if he would be her prince. She thought about the Day of her wedding often. The Day when she'd be held by someone, when she'd be taken into two arms forever and find deep, safe, expansive pasture for her soul at last. She wrote of that Day often in her secret diary and always locked her tender dreams safely away with that thin metal key. She treasured her little diary and all it contained.

"This gal I knew, she grew up with the normal fears and hesitations and doubts of a little girl. Was there a glory about her creation? Was that strange man on the other side of the restaurant going to stop staring at her? Would anything happen when she walked home from school today?

"And this gal I knew thought of that Day when she'd be held by two arms. And she dated. And wondered. And spent hours looking in the mirror. And the fears and hesitations and doubts swirled around her, haunted her. Like every little girl who looks into the mirror for an hour.

"This gal I knew did marry. That Day came. And on that Day all the fears and hesitations lost their grip on her and she allowed herself to melt into the moment and into his arms. She changed her name, and every time she heard this new name, it surprised her and she was reminded afresh of her new identity and how the fears and hesitations and doubts no longer had control over her. And she felt his arms around her."

THE DIRTY BEGGAR swallows at this point, as if he had gotten a bad taste in his mouth. His face grimaces slightly as he continues to talk.

"Early one afternoon this gal I knew was in her bedroom, stooping over, gathering all the dirty laundry from the floor of the closet. And she picked up the dark blue button-up shirt she had bought for her husband for his birthday—the shirt that made him look so tall and so crisp and so strong— and she indulged, burying her face in the shirt and breathing in deeply, slowly to smell him and think of him and feel near to him.

"But this gal I knew didn't smell her husband that early afternoon on the floor of her bedroom. She smelled perfume. A different perfume from her own. It was the smell of another woman that she inhaled from that shirt.

"And the tender moment of indulgence and intimacy was invaded by sharp, dark, grabbing feelings. The old fears perked up and the old hesitations and doubts sat up and took notice. But they had lost their power, their tight grip. His arms that Day, this covenant of forever, was a fence, a tall fence that had created safe pastures for her soul. And the shady fears lurked around the fence but did not come into the pastures of her soul.

"But then this gal I knew, she smelled that perfume a few more times while doing the laundry. And a few times his arms held her differently and his eyes would look away. And then this gal I knew saw him sitting with her at a restaurant. With *her,* the other woman. She saw him looking into her eyes. And his arm reached across the cheap red-and-white checked tablecloth and his hand touched hers. His hand touched *hers*.

"And in that one moment—in those few seconds staring through the cheap Italian restaurant's window—the tall, strong walls of safety crumbled and the evil fears and doubts and hesitations raided the soft pastures of her soul with mud on their boots. With their dark, twisted bodies, this blur of evil came into her and attacked and slapped and grabbed with the vigor of an army that has rested for years just waiting for the chance to raid and pillage and rape and seize.

"And this was just in that moment of seeing his hand touch hers."

THE DIRTY BEGGAR's eyes are closed at this point. He is hugging his legs to his chest, rocking slightly. His face low to the ground, half hidden in his robe. After long moments of silence, the other ideas in my head staring at him all the while, he continues rasping out his low, deep story . . .

"There was more after that moment. For this gal I knew, there were the lies from him as he looked into her eyes, the embarrassing letter she had to write to the family, the bitter days in court, the nights of having to sleep alone in that queen-sized bed, the having to start living again with a raided soul, under the tight grip of the fears and hesitations and doubts with their muddy boots roaming around the damaged pastures of her soul.

"And this gal I knew—she's his daughter. The Father's daughter. She belongs to God.

"And He saw everything. He sat as a Father, breathing in the glory of her creation, the beauty of her soul, the rightness of the safety of those arms and that covenant on that Day when she changed her name. And the eyes of this Father watched the dark, evil, murderous invasion of adultery. He saw the invasion of her tender soul.

"And his fist did pull back. There is wrath in the fist in his stomach. And that wrath is pure and right. Choices have consequences and his fist must fly."

The ideas sitting in the living room in my head listening to THE DIRTY BEGGAR's story are quieter afterward. They are not sure what to say at this point. This kind of silence, still and near, in the living room up in my head is rare. Eventually THE DIRTY BEGGAR living in my head says a little more.

"I've known lots of people, you know. Lots of people.

"Our eyes are clouded over, blurred up a lot, you see. And so we only see the most obvious, the most cartoonish sins. Like . . . like with a kid. With a kid, it's easier for our blurred-up eyes to see the glory of their creation. The beauty of who they are and the rightness of how they should be embraced and treated."

THE DIRTY BEGGAR closes his eyes and is silent for a moment before continuing.

"So when we hear about some man touching a little kid with thick fingers, we *feel* the wrath. It doesn't even have to be your own kid—it's obvious, isn't it? The disparity between the glory and the evil is just so obvious. We read of these horrors in the morning paper while eating breakfast and our own stomach fists pull back. With us maybe it's not a completely righteous fist, but it's close to it."

THE DIRTY BEGGAR looks up for a moment, his eyes staring ahead as if he is watching a scene intently, carefully.

"But then we laugh at adultery. We treat it so lightly, so casually. Rape a kid, you go to jail; commit adultery, you fit in. And so we buy that stupid fool's twisted story about a 'spectrum' of sins. What a load of crap!"

THE DIRTY BEGGAR's voice is even more hoarse from the talking. But he pushes his deep, scarred voice and continues to talk.

"We only see what's obvious, because our eyes are so . . . dull. So when a kid is sinned against, we see it more clearly. Or when someone close to us is sinned against, we see it clearly as well. In fact, I think the closer someone is to us, the more clearly we see the glory of them and the more clearly we see the evil reach of sins against them no matter what the sin.

"Yeah. The closer someone is to us, the more clearly we feel our stomach fists rightly pull back. The more we know the fist must fly, that dark choices have real consequences.

"But God . . . oh, he sees everything. He sees *everything*. He sees the glory of it all. They are his daughters and sons, every one. And he loves them, every one. They are so close to him. Every one. He breathes in the glory of them all. God *is* love.

"And God sees everything. He sees every dark scrape of sin, no matter where the claw comes from. He sees the dark invasion of adultery—and what it does to his daughter's soul. He sees his son being lied to—and the deep, slashing sword swing into his son's heart that it is. He sees his daughter being shamed by her jealous friends in the mall—and the thousands of thick-fingered fists of shame that pound upon her with a deep, relentless, silent pounding. He even sees the icicle torture of indifference. He sees the sharp icicle of indifference being plunged again and again, jabbed into his young son's soul.

"Dull human eyes may be mostly blind to these dark claws and the damage they bring to his children. But not so with God. He sees it all. And because he loves his children deeply, intimately, his fist is pulled back. And it must fly.

"And there is nowhere, nowhere to hide."

Chapter 5

THE DAY OF JUDGMENT

Many of the ideas up in my head are not used to being around an idea like this strange, shy, dirty beggar. He's very serious. And usually so very quiet.

And yet when he does talk, it's often in these stories that make you feel weird inside. Some of the new ideas that come into my head from time to time are shocked to see him in there. He changes the mood of the room. I'm sure you know people like that. You sometimes wish they'd go away. That's what this dirty beggar is like up in my head.

After his stories about adultery and such, many of the ideas wish he *would* just go away, but he doesn't. So, many of them leave my head instead. THE FINGERLESS LADY, ABOVE ALL NEVER JUDGE, TRUTH IS RELATIVE—these and other ideas can't stand to be in the room with him. So they have to leave my head. I can tell they can't believe I let such a pointy idea stay living in my head.

POINTING IS RUDE stands perplexed—he doesn't know what to do with someone who is pointing *at himself.* Eventually POINTING IS RUDE walks out of my head too, not able to stand the looks of that dirty beggar and the sound of his harsh, pointing words. A house wants order, after all. And living ideas that don't get along will work out their tension—or one of them will leave. And many do leave after hearing these strange stories and odd conclusions from THE DIRTY BEGGAR living in my head.

But some ideas stick around. They have more questions for him.

RELAX, STUFF HAPPENS sits up straight from his usually slouched position and looks over at THE DIRTY BEGGAR. "Listen, I appreciate your stories. They are very touching." Some ideas roll their eyes at this point. "But if people really are supposed to be bent over and feeling guilty like you because of their sins, then why doesn't it happen?"

THE DIRTY BEGGAR looks up and clears his throat. "Why doesn't *what* happen?"

RELAX, STUFF HAPPENS shrugs his shoulders. "You know—judgment. Wrath. The swinging of that infamous fist. Your stories . . . well, they hold no weight—because it just doesn't happen. Good things happen to bad people, bad things happen to good people. If our misdeeds really did make God's fist rightly pull back as a natural consequence, then why don't people feel it?"

HUMANISM nods at this point and looks to the

lowly idea crouched over on the ground. He starts to feel a little sorry for him and wonders when I'll finally kick that poor beggar out of my mind for good.

But THE DIRTY BEGGAR looks up at HUMANISM and RELAX, STUFF HAPPENS, slowly looks each idea in the eye, and says, "Patience. His patience. The day will come."

YOUTHFUL CYNICISM sighs loudly and shakes his head, his long, dark bangs swaying from side to side over his sad eyes. "What day? And do you happen to know when that day is going to be?"

"That Day. The day of judgment."

"What?!" YOUTHFUL CYNICISM smiles and looks around at the other ideas living in my head before continuing in his sarcastic tones. "Do you mean when we're standing at the Pearly Gates and St. Peter is checking his scroll to see if we're on the guest list?" Lots of smiles from the ideas living in my head.

THE DIRTY BEGGAR just sits, looking at each of the ideas around him. And then he slowly begins to nod, looking back at YOUTHFUL CYNICISM. "I'm not so sure about the gates and St. Peter, though. But, yeah, you're right. Isn't he?" At this THE DIRTY BEGGAR looks over at THE OLD MAN.

THE OLD MAN CLUTCHING THE BIG BLACK BIBLE nods and starts flipping through the large, thin, yellowed pages until he finds the page he's looking for. "Jesus went through the towns and villages, teaching as he made his way to Jerusalem. Someone asked him, 'Lord, are only a few people going to be saved?' He said to them, 'Make every effort to enter through the narrow door, because many, I tell you, will try to enter and will not be able to. Once the owner of the house gets up and closes the door, you will stand outside knocking and . . . say, "We ate and drank with you, and you taught in our streets." But he will reply, "I don't know you or where you come from. Away from me, all you evildoers!" There will be weeping there, and gnashing of teeth, when you see Abraham, Isaac and Jacob and all the prophets in the kingdom of God, but you yourselves thrown out. People will come from east and west and north and south, and will take their places at the feast in the kingdom of God.'"[1] THE OLD MAN looks up from the page and nods at THE DIRTY BEGGAR.

TRUTH IS RELATIVE (who's come back into my head, not willing to give up so easily), THE CHURCH IS BANKRUPT (AND HAS HURT ME) and HUMANISM just stare at THE OLD MAN when he makes this point. YOUTHFUL CYNICISM isn't sure what to say. So, as usual, THE OLD MAN fills the silence with the soft sound of ancient pages being turned, and he reads from the big black book in his arms. "Jesus told the people around him at one point, 'I tell you, my friends, do not be afraid of those who kill the body and after that can do no more. But I will show you whom you should fear: Fear him who, after your body has been killed, has authority to throw you into hell. Yes, I tell you, fear him.' "[2]

There's still silence in my head. (Many new ideas up in my head can't get used to this old guy's reading; they just stare at him and his old book, incredulous.) So after flipping several more pages, the crinkling of the old pages filling the silence of the room, THE OLD MAN starts reading again. "Another time Jesus told his followers this: 'Again, the kingdom of heaven is like a net that was let down into the lake and caught all kinds of fish. When it was full, the fishermen pulled it up on the shore. Then they sat down and collected the good fish in baskets, but threw the bad away. This is how it will be at the end of the age. The angels will come and separate the wicked from the righteous and throw them into the blazing furnace, where there will be weeping and gnashing of teeth.' "[3]

THE OLD MAN continues, looking at the ideas standing around in my head. "Jesus told many parables like this—always with the same ending: a great day of judgment. Weeds and plants being separated, and the weeds being put into eternal fires. Sheep and goats being separated, and the goats being sent out to eternal punishment. A great banquet being held, and some people let in while others are shut out."

THE OLD MAN stops reading and sits there, holding his big black book and nodding slowly, blinking thoughtfully.

THE DIRTY BEGGAR's hoarse voice is heard again, though he doesn't look up from the floor. "It's coming, you know. The fist *is* pulled back. And it must fly. I know. I have a sister, like I told you already. I know that it must fly, because I have a sister and her hands are thin. And . . . and he sees everything. And Jesus promised that all of history will come to a day of reckoning. A great day of accounting, of consequences."

The beggar looks around at the ideas around him, his eyes growing wild again. "We are all . . . we . . ." He looks around as if he is about to jump up and start screaming. But the moment passes and he simply looks down at the ground in front of him again. "I have done it. I am . . . I am . . . What was it that THE OLD MAN read about me? There was something about me in that book of his."

THE DIRTY BEGGAR closes his eyes tightly. Eventually he begins nodding, and almost in a whisper, as if reciting an oath, he continues speaking— each word sputtered separately, slowly. "You are storing up wrath against yourself for the day of God's wrath, when his righteous judgment will be revealed."[4]

THE DIRTY BEGGAR up in my head starts to

shake his head slowly. He looks up, his eyes—his bloodshot, pained eyes—look at RELAX, STUFF HAPPENS and IT'S ALL OK and WHAT A WONDER-FUL WORLD as they casually slouch in a nearby couch. THE DIRTY BEGGAR looks them in the eyes, his head still shaking slowly. "No, sir. It is not OK. It is most definitely not going to be OK. The Day will come and a right, pure, strong fist will strike. Just one solid, eternal blow. And there's nowhere I can hide."

There is an intensity in THE DIRTY BEGGAR's eyes and his voice seems stronger than it has been, though still just as desperate. "No one can hide on that day. We will be face to face then." His head stops shaking and slowly starts nodding up and down.

His whole body starts to rock slowly back and forth, slowly back and forth. "I have stored up wrath. I have so much stored up. And his righteous fist will be revealed. It will be revealed as it swings into my guilty, dirty face."

After THE DIRTY BEGGAR living in my head re-cites his oath of guilt, he sits quietly.

The living room in my head, where ideas come to talk and hear each other's stories and work it all out, is quiet. It is so rarely this quiet.

Eventually MIDDLE-CLASS SPIRITUALITY, an av-erage-looking idea, speaks into the silence. "OK, Mr. Moody. Even if we buy that there's not a spectrum of sins, and that every sin is deserving of hell (which I am not saying I'm buying!), and even if we buy that it hasn't happened yet because God's waiting patiently for this one Day to come, there's still the fact that some people are worse than others. When I look around this little world, I see all sorts of people who are much more mean and hurtful and *sinful* than others. You've gotta admit that."

THE DIRTY BEGGAR living in my head looks up at this point. "Admit what?"

MIDDLE-CLASS SPIRITUALITY continues in his calm voice. "That if God has some system where regular folks and serial murderers end up getting the same punishment, the system is messed up. And that your story becomes hard to believe. Really hard to believe."

Many of the ideas in my head start to nod thoughtfully, and MIDDLE-CLASS SPIRITUALITY smiles as he continues. "Sure, not everyone's a saint like Mother Teresa, but not everyone's a monster who goes around raping kids either. You just can't break it all up, black and white. It's not like that. How can it just be Door One (welcome to the feast) or Door Two (go sizzle in the fire)? There's nothing commonsensical or right or fair about that. It's old-fashioned and unbelievable. Sure, it's fine for putting fear into kids, but it's an unrealistic story."

"Unrealistic?" THE DIRTY BEGGAR sounds like

he has something caught in his throat and should cough. But he doesn't. He just stares up at MIDDLE-CLASS SPIRITUALITY.

"Yeah, unrealistic. Where's room for the spiritual *middle class*, those who aren't saints or monsters? Just regular people who've done some wrong stuff but aren't destroying the world or anything. Your story about judgment day just doesn't make sense for those in the middle. Those in the real world."

THE DIRTY BEGGAR living in my head looks up at this point, with a curious look in his bloodshot eyes. "Spiritual *middle class*?" He actually smiles at this point, a rare thing. But, as it turns out, his twisted smile is really nothing to look at. "Can I tell you about these guys I knew?"

Some of the ideas in the living room in my head, growing tired of the conversation, look at their watches and wonder when I am going to finally kick this silly, depressed beggar guy out. But, feeling committed (and perhaps seeing my inaction), they sit down, resigned to hear one more sob story.

So THE DIRTY BEGGAR in my head starts to tell another story with his hoarse, unsophisticated voice.

"I knew these two guys once. I knew them well. And so do you."

With these words he gives the whole room a look that is unmistakable. Every idea up there now knows this is going to be a story from my own life. And every idea knows that stories from my own experience carry a lot of weight up in the living room of my head (they really affect how I think). So most of the ideas perk up at this, their eyes growing wider. They lean in as THE DIRTY BEGGAR drones his story out in a deep, raspy voice . . .

"These two guys I knew were brothers and were regular guys, like everyone else. They grew up making friends and losing friends and going to school and climbing trees. They ate baloney sandwiches and caught baby turtles in the grass and memorized the multiplication tables. They thrilled in opening Christmas presents and laughed at jokes and were made fun of and made fun of others. Just regular kids.

"They ran through the woods together, singing brave, catchy tunes from Army commercials they had seen on the black-and-white TV in their house. They stole money and bought cigarettes at a country store and hid in the chicken coop and smoked them. Then they drank lemonade to try and hide the smell when they went back into the house. They played on frozen ponds in the winter and snuck into unkempt fields and rode bareback on dirty horses, holding onto the rough black manes to stay on.

"They rode bikes together and played basketball together and explored underneath the bleachers while waiting for the next game at the gym. They climbed hundreds of trees and swung on vines in the dense, green foothills of the Appalachian Mountains. They made good choices and bad choices. They loved people and were mean to people. Regular guys. Two brothers, they were. Not far apart in age.

"One day these two guys I knew moved apart from each other. They didn't see each other for years. They didn't write or call or e-mail. They lived their own lives, you see.

"When they met again, after years without contact, they were both adults. They weren't little boys anymore. And they seemed different from each other now. Very different. One brother was a convicted child molester; the other brother was a pastor.

"When the pastor found out where his brother was being held, he booked a plane ticket immediately and flew out to see his long-lost brother. The two brothers were going to look into each other's eyes for the first time in years. On the airplane the pastor slept fitfully, his dreams crowded with images of little green turtles and silver basketball bleachers and dirty horses and frozen ponds.

"If you had seen the pastor reading on the plane or taking the light rail to a hotel near the jail, you might have described him as a 'saint.' Rushing to the coast to see his brother. Preparing a sermon in the airport lounge for the coming Sunday. Carefully making a list of topics he would like to talk about with his brother the next day. Thoughtful, careful, selfless. A saint if ever there was one in this country.

"If you had seen the convicted brother waiting in his cell, you might have been tempted to spit at him. A tortured look on his face from the guilt of years of ripping the innocence away from young boys and thrusting into their lives a legacy of shame and fear and confusion and twisted understandings. An evil, unthinkable past. And a suicidal, desperate present: one shower a week, a bent pair of glasses that were the wrong prescription, a six-by-ten-foot cell, infamy and shame in the media, threatening looks from the eyes of other prisoners. A dark, confusing, crashing present.

"An evil past, a desperate present and an uncertain future. If you wouldn't call him a 'monster' just by looking at him (which you very well might), reading one article about his crimes, looking once into the eyes of his victims, contemplating even for a moment what he had done to these boys would fully convince you that he was a monster.

"The saint fell asleep peacefully in his warm hotel room, surrounded by his books and sermon notes. The monster went to sleep fitfully, surrounded by the ruins of an evil life.

"But an interesting thing happened when the sun came up.

"The two brothers did look into each other's eyes—through a thick window of glass. And they did talk—through the static of cheap jail phones. And they asked each other questions. And laughed. And were brothers.

"And the saint was surprised to find out how kind and thoughtful and compassionate and . . . *saintly* the monster could be—just like when he was a kid. And the monster was surprised to find out how complicated and selfish and careless and . . . *monstrous* the saint could be—just like when he was a kid.

"The world kept its labels, seeing one brother as a saint and the other as a monster. But the two brothers knew something different. They knew something that not everyone knew. They had a secret.

THE DIRTY BEGGAR pauses, whispers, "They were surprised to find out that there are no saints and there are no monsters."

At this THE DIRTY BEGGAR living in my head stops. Tired of speaking. Not used to the attention from so many ideas. Many of the ideas living in my head just stare at him. Stories from my life hold a lot of weight up there in that head of mine, and every idea knows that.

The story reverberates through my mind. And that perfectly commonsense, very popular idea, MIDDLE-CLASS SPIRITUALITY, is nowhere to be seen.

Even SELF-HATRED, that skinny, lanky idea who had started creeping out of his dark corner when THE DIRTY BEGGAR started telling his dark stories, looks deflated again by this new story. SELF-HATRED is unsure of whether he needs to hide away again or whether this dirty beggar will be a friend to him after all. SELF-HATRED stands, unsure, at the back of the crowd.

The silence fills my head until the rough voice of THE DIRTY BEGGAR speaks again.

"I've met a lot of people, I'll tell you that. I've known lots of guys. Lots of gals. But I'll tell you something—I've never met a saint. And I've never met a monster. Read about them plenty in fairy tales and stories, but I've never met one. Plenty of monstrous, saintly regular people. But that's the only kind of person I've ever met."

There's more awkward silence in my head at this point as the ideas living up there try to figure out how to proceed. THE OLD MAN CLUTCHING THE BIG BLACK BIBLE chimes in and reads a few verses from that ancient book of his. "There's a saint in everyone, you know. Right here at the beginning of this book we read, 'Then God said, let us make human beings in our image, in our likeness. . . . And it was so. God saw all that he had made, and it was very good.' "[5]

A saint in everyone? At these words SELF-HATRED cringes and starts slinking back to his closet. But

THE OLD MAN flips some more of the thin pages of his book and continues, with a different tone in his voice, "And there's a monster there too. It says here, 'If we say that we have no sin, we deceive ourselves, and the truth is not in us,' 'for all have sinned and fall short of the glory of God.' "[6]

The hoarse voice of THE DIRTY BEGGAR living in my head interrupts THE OLD MAN at this point. "You know, guys, every person ever judged is a monstrous saint or a saintly monster. Every one. That's regular life. That's middle class. We're all a mix of rags and jewels. We're all rich in the glory of our creation, and we're also very, very poor."

His eyes close at this point and his face drops slowly back to the ground. "That's the only kind of people I've ever met."

THE DIRTY BEGGAR's rough voice sounds faraway. "And that's the only kind of people who stand before God on the day of judgment. There are no saints to welcome in and no monsters to kick away. There are just regular folks with rags and jewels. And a sure, right fist."

Chapter 6

IN THE PATH OF
THE FIST

If you could see the confusion and chaos in my head at this point, you'd understand why THE DIRTY BEGGAR rarely wants to tell his story. And why he rarely gets permission to tell the whole thing.

All ideas have a story to tell. But Pointy Ideas rarely get a fair hearing. And this story is one of the pointiest stories I have ever allowed to remain in my head.[1] It's an uncomfortable idea. And what it tells me about the darkness and evil in this world, and most specifically about my part in that, is a story that disrupts the comfort of my life.

There are some days when I am tired of this beggar's stories. I think he is dark and he exaggerates. I think he is old-fashioned and depressed. I look around at the soft, suburban world I walk through, and nothing seems quite as desperate and harsh as he makes it out to be. And when I compare myself to other folks around me, I don't seem to be doing so bad. Mostly applause and pats on the back are what I get from other folks. This makes such an idea about my own guilt and the dirt on my own hands and these eternal consequences seem over the top. On those days THE DIRTY BEGGAR's talk of my guilt and the reality of hell seem like so much irrelevant theology.

There are other days, though, when something happens that gives me a window into another person, or helps me feel the weight of my own soul, and I can't help but think he is onto something.

I feel the rightness of his lowly, guilty posture. It feels strangely right as I reflect on my own life and my own actions. And my own darkness. His posture fits. And I sit, thoughtful, and know my own guilt, the dirt that is on my hands. And I know that I have no defense, that actions have consequences and that I deserve wrath. My soul bows silently, just like that beggar. And in the stillness of my own confession, I sense the realness of his story.

In the end, I just like his story. And I like the answers he gives in the living room. I like the fact that THE OLD MAN seems to agree with him. (THE OLD MAN has seniority status up there, after all.) And after seeing him go a few rounds in the living room, I like how he responds to the other ideas living up in my head.

I sense truth in his story. It resonates more and fits more than some of the softer, sugar ideas up there. And so, in the end, I let him stay. I believe this idea. I believe I am guilty. I believe I have scratched darkness into the world and that this has consequences.

THE DIRTY BEGGAR isn't the only idea living up there that tells me about the darkness in this world, of course. THERE IS A HIDDEN SPIRITUAL LANDSCAPE! is still up there. And I believe her story about dark spiritual beings that breathe on people and push the world to darker and darker places. I believe ORIGINAL SIN and what he tells me about a dark disease that we're all born with.

These ideas have no problem living in the same head with THE DIRTY BEGGAR. Some of the other ideas up there, though, aren't thrilled to be so close to such a dark, self-implicating idea. Many of the other ideas in my head leave before he gets his full story out. They can't stand being in a head that believes such things about evil and hell.

But especially after that last bit about monsters and saints, there is real chaos up in my head. HUMANISM and YOUTHFUL CYNICISM are outright laughing at THE DIRTY BEGGAR, pointing at him and mocking him. POINTING IS RUDE and ABOVE ALL NEVER JUDGE are disgusted. INTEGRITY is sitting quietly, brows furrowed.

Usually, in the midst of all this chaos, a question or two is lobbed toward THE DIRTY BEGGAR. And when there's enough of a pause, sometimes he'll try to answer.

HUMANISM (who had been whispering for a moment with INTEGRITY) lifts his popular, strong voice above the din of the crowd. "Do you realize, Mr. Depressed, that if the story you are telling us is true, then there's no hope for anyone? If every person is a monster, at least in part, and if this means they've done things that incur God's *righteous wrath* (quite a phrase, by the way!), then everyone is going to get smashed by this great God of yours when they reach the Pearly Gates. What a story you've got there!"

Usually chaos reigns again after such a comment, followed by many shouts from other ideas. They're calling for THE DIRTY BEGGAR to be thrown out. These other ideas plead with me. Many of them don't think they can live under the same roof with a dirty, depressed idea like this anymore.

Sometimes GOD IS LOVE will try one last time to persuade THE DIRTY BEGGAR to give up such stories about God. "Don't you realize, son, that the way you're talking makes God come off as a really mean, wrathful guy? I like it when you speak of him as a Father—I think you're onto something there. But why such talk of a fist? God is so full of love and affection; how could he ever ball up his hand in a fist toward his children and leave them defenseless? How could . . ."

GOD IS LOVE trails off when she realizes THE DIRTY BEGGAR isn't listening anymore. He is nodding slowly and looking across the living room of my head directly at another idea. GOD IS LOVE follows his gaze to the idea he's staring at.

That idea is a tall, beautiful woman who's smiling at THE DIRTY BEGGAR. She's plainly dressed. Simple hair. No makeup. But her beauty is at once striking and her eyes . . . well, her eyes bring her beauty right into your very head and make you feel more awake than you ever have. And you find yourself staring at her smiling lips and wishing she would speak.

The other ideas living in my head are mostly quiet now. GOD IS LOVE asks THE DIRTY BEGGAR in a whisper, "Who is she? What kind of story does she tell?"

THE DIRTY BEGGAR's gaze is steady and almost calm. His voice still has a painful rasping quality to it, though, like someone in the desert who hasn't had a drink in days. "That idea over there? That smiling woman has the best story of all." The beggar's gaze does not fall from her, though he grows quiet and thoughtful.

"But what is her story?" GOD IS LOVE finds herself staring at the tall, beautiful idea.

"She tells a story about . . . about one who walks into the path of the fist."

"Into the path of the fist?"

THE DIRTY BEGGAR nods, his eyes never leaving the woman's gaze. "She tells how the fist is right.

And how there is one who steps right into its path, to take the pounding of God's fist into his very own face."

GOD IS LOVE cringes at this and gazes over at the smiling, beautiful woman. THERE IS A HIDDEN SPIRITUAL LANDSCAPE! is gazing over at the woman as well. As is ORIGINAL SIN and many of the other ideas about darkness that live up in my head. Their eyes look into hers and calmness settles into them.

YOUTHFUL CYNICISM looks down at THE DIRTY BEGGAR and scoffs, "It would take a desperate idea like you to believe a far-fetched story like that!" And with that, many of the ideas living in my head walk away from THE DIRTY BEGGAR. They can't believe I let such an old-fashioned idea stay living up there in my head. As they are leaving the living room in my head, these ideas try to avoid the eyes of the smiling woman.

But other ideas, including GOD IS LOVE, look from the desperate beggar to the smiling woman, and back again.

CONCLUSION:
YOUR HEAD

....

If your head works anything like mine, then by your reading this book, THE DIRTY BEGGAR has walked into your head as well. Ideas are like that: like people who come into your head and interact with all the other ideas living there. So, um . . . THE DIRTY BEGGAR's living in your head now too. Or at least visiting.

Maybe you're ready to kick him out right now. Maybe you hear the whistles and barked comments from some of the other ideas in your mind already as they catch sight of this miserable, bent-over idea. My advice is this: let 'em work it out. Even if you're not used to an idea that tells such seemingly dark, strange stories that could ruin the mood in the living room in your head.

Even unpopular, old-fashioned ideas have a story to tell. Every idea does. Let the ideas tell each other their stories. Pepper *them all* with questions. And see how things shake out.

That's what we've been given brains for, after all. To think. To let the ideas work it out as we bring them all into the living room of our minds and ask them to interact with each other.

But remember, it's your head. It's your house of living ideas. No one in there gets to boss other ideas around—without your permission. No one gets to stay, no one has to leave, without your say-so.

So work it out. This is the job of humans—to philosophize, to think, to be in charge of our heads. THE DIRTY BEGGAR has gone and walked right into the house of your head. He's in there now. It's up to you to figure out what to do with him.

It's your head, after all.

NOTES

introduction: my head

[1]To get a more comprehensive view of how things work up in my head, you'd have to read *All the Ideas Living in My Head: One Guy's Musings About Truth,* where I give a full tour of my upstairs and how thinking tends to go on up there. It's a tell-all about how ideas behave in my head, the different types of ideas there are, why certain ideas get special privileges, how my mind interacts with my heart and soul, how I talk with others about their ideas and what, exactly, I think about McDonald's French fries. Among other things.

chapter 2: the dirty beggar's story

[1]THE OLD MAN CLUTCHING THE BIG BLACK BIBLE (an important idea who lives up in my head and whom you'll meet officially a little later on) reads to me about such prowling. For example, 1 Peter 5:8.

[2]THE OLD MAN reads me plenty of stuff about this, such as Ephesians 6:10-12. Pretty thought-provoking stuff on a day when you're sitting around and contemplating darkness.

[3]For more on this and other shocking "secret ideas" that live in my head, you can read *All the Ideas Living in My Head,* chapter four.

chapter 4: rapists one and all

[1]This idea is pretty active up in the living room of my head—he affects a lot of my thinking. He's a member of the Enlightenment Gang, and you can read more about him in *All the Ideas Living in My Head* and *The Old Man Living in My Head*. He's quite funny to look at (no one really goes around wearing tight jumpsuits anymore) but is a powerful idea.

[2]For more on this old fellow and his story, read *The Old Man Living in My Head: One Guy's Musings About the Bible*.

[3]Matthew 5:21-30

[4]James 2:8-13

[5]Mark 7:20-23

[6]Matthew 18:6

chapter 5: the day of judgment

[1]Luke 13:22-29

[2]Luke 12:4-5

[3]Matthew 13:47-50

[4]Romans 2:5

[5]Genesis 1:26,30-31 NRSV

[6]1 John 1:8 NRSV; Romans 3:23

chapter 6: in the path of the fist

[1]As explained in the initial tour of how thinking happens up in my head *(All the Ideas Living in My Head: One Guy's Musings About Truth),* some ideas are "pointy," which means they make life uncomfortable for me. This is in contrast to Sugar Ideas, who tell stories that I just know will make my life easier, whether they are good stories or not.

ONE GUY'S HEAD SERIES

A bunch of ideas are running around in Don Everts's head. Some are permanent residents. Others are visitors, just passing through. When they all get together, some odd things start happening.

All the Ideas Living in My Head: One Guy's Musings About Truth, ISBN: 978-0-8308-3611-6

The Old Man Living in My Head: One Guy's Musings About the Bible, ISBN: 978-0-8308-3612-3

The Dirty Beggar Living in My Head: One Guy's Musings About Evil & Hell, ISBN: 978-0-8308-3613-0

The Fingerless Lady Living in My Head: One Guy's Musings About Tolerance, ISBN: 978-0-8308-3614-7

LIKEWISE. *Go and do.*

....

A man comes across an ancient enemy, beaten and left for dead. He lifts the wounded man onto the back of a donkey and takes him to an inn to tend to the man's recovery. Jesus tells this story and instructs those who are listening to "go and do likewise."

Likewise books explore a compassionate, active faith lived out in real time. When we're skeptical about the status quo, Likewise books challenge us to create culture responsibly. When we're confused about who we are and what we're supposed to be doing, Likewise books help us listen for God's voice. When we're discouraged by the troubled world we've inherited, Likewise books encourage us to hold onto hope.

In this life we will face challenges that demand our response. Likewise books face those challenges with us so we can act on faith.

....

likewisebooks.com

....